.1

THE MAYAS
(ON THE ROCKS)

BY:
JAVIER COVO T.

Dante

Producción Editorial Dante, S.A.

THE MAYAS (On the Rocks)
Javier Covo T.

1ª Ed. Coleccioón "MONO-GRAMAS": 1987

© Producción Editorial Dante, S. A.
   Calle 59 # 472
   Mérida, Yucatán, México.
   C.P. 97000

Queda hecho el depósito que marca la ley.
I.S.B.N. 968-7232-63-3

Diseño: Javier Covo T.

Traducción: Gustavo Fernández, Ph.D.

IMPRESO EN MEXICO
PRINTED IN MEXICO

TO ESTEBAN...
SLEEPLESS YUCATECAN...
(AND MY SON BY THE WAY).

THE TERRITORY OF THE MAYA

THE TERRITORY INHABITED BY THE MAYA COVERS ABOUT 154,507 SQUARED MILES (400,000 SQ. KM.) IT EXTENDED OVER WHAT TODAY ARE THE MEXICAN STATES OF YUCATAN, CAMPECHE, QUINTANA ROO AND PARTS OF CHIAPAS AND TABASCO; BELICE AND GUATEMALA AND REGIONS OF HONDURAS AND EL SALVADOR IN CENTRAL AMERICA.

LET'S DIVIDE THE MAYA AREA IN THREE ZONES FOR A BETTER UNDERSTANDING.

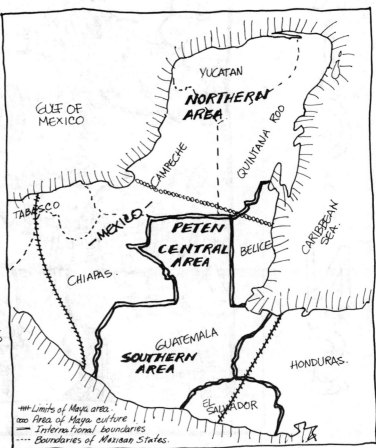

GULF OF MEXICO

YUCATAN

NORTHERN AREA

CAMPECHE

QUINTANA ROO

TABASCO

MEXICO

PETEN CENTRAL AREA

BELICE

CARIBBEAN SEA.

CHIAPAS.

GUATEMALA

SOUTHERN AREA

HONDURAS.

EL SALVADOR

⊬⊬⊬ Limits of Maya area.
ᴏᴏᴏ Area of Maya culture
═══ International boundaries
----- Boundaries of Mexican States.

1:- THE NORTH, COMPRISES THE MEXICAN STATES OF YUCATAN, QUINTANA ROO AND MOST OF CAMPECHE.

2:- THE CENTRAL, INCLUDES THE PETEN IN GUATEMALA AND ADJACENT REGIONS.

3:- THE SOUTH, FORMED BY PARTS OF CHIAPAS (MEXICO), GUATEMALA, EL SALVADOR AND HONDURAS.

THE ORIGINS

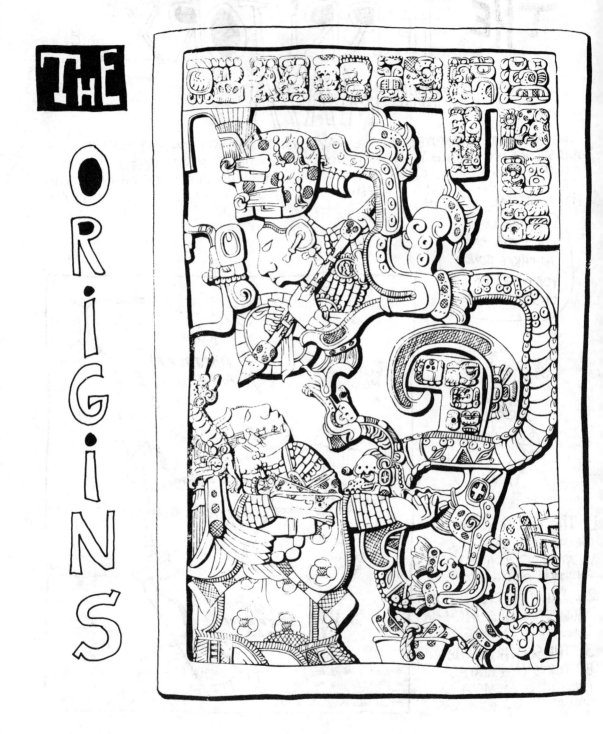

WHAT ARE WE?
WHERE DO WE COME FROM?
WHERE WILL WE GO?

THEY WERE AS LOST AS MEXICAN ECONOMY

SCHOLARS, RESEARCHERS AND ORIGINALISTS AFTER YEARS OF HARD WORK HAVE SHED LITTLE IF ANY LIGHT OVER THIS MATTER.

DUE TO CERTAIN PHYSICAL CHARACTERISTICS LIKE THE ICE CUBE SHAPE OF THE HEAD. SOME ANTROPOLOGISTS HAVE HIPOTHE- -SIZED THAT THE MAYA PEOPLE PROCEED FROM ASIA.

SAY WHAT YOU WISH, BUT BETWEEN 2000 BC. AND 1000 A.D. WE WERE ALREADY HERE.

ABOUT 1000 YEARS BEFORE CHRIST AGRICUL- -TURE HAD ENVOLVED AMONG MESOAMERICAN PEOPLE AND THEY POSSESSED UNIFORM CULTURE AT LEAST IN 328 AD. THERE EXISTED A DATED "ESTELA" IN UAXACTUN.

THE HISTORIC AGES OF THE MAYA ARE:

PRECLASSIC
- INFERIOR (1500 BC. - 800 BC.)
- MEDIUM (800 BC. - 300 BC.)
- SUPERIOR (300 BC. - 150 BC.)

CLASSIC
- PROTOCLASSIC (150 BC. - 300 AD.)
- EARLY CLASSIC (300 AD. - 600 AD.)
- LATE CLASSIC (600 AD. - 900 A.D.)

ABOUT THIS TIME THE MAYA CULTURE, PARTICULARY AT PALENQUE UNEXPECTEDLY COLLAPSED ALMOST TO ASHES.

(AT THIS MOMENT, IN EUROPE, CHARLES THE MAGNE REIGNED OVER THE CHRISTIAN WORLD).

POST-CLASSIC
- EARLY (1000 AD - 1250 AD.)
- LATE (1250 AD. - 1541 AD.)

13

THE PRECLASSIC PERIOD.

INFERIOR PRECLASSIC:
(1500 BC. - 800 BC.)

ABOUT 1000 BC, THE MAYA PEOPLE BEGAN CULTIVATING LAND IN A PRIMITIVE AGRICULTURE... THEY LIVED IN HAMLETS, SURVIVING THANKS TO A SELFSUFICIENT ECONOMY.

SUCH WAS LIFE

CORN ABOUNDED LETTING PEOPLE TO SEDENTARIZE.

MEDIUM PRECLASSIC
(800 BC. - 300 BC.)

THE SMART ONES STARTED TO GROW "SUPERNATURAL POWERS" AND COMAND OVER THE REST. PRIEST, CHAMAN AND CLEREGYMEN WERE THE FIRST SMARTERS.

OLMECS CAME BRINGING WRITING AND CALENDAR WITH THEM.

THE FIRST CRAFTS TO FLOWER UP WERE **CERAMIC** AND **BASKET MAKING.**

SUPERIOR PRECLASSIC :
(300 BC. - 150 AD.)

WIZARDS AND CHAMANS BECAME "GODS' HEARERS" AND LATELY EXPLOITERS OF THE PEOPLE.

TWO TYPES OF MEN ALREADY EXISTED, THE ONE WHO HOLDS THE PACKAGE AND THE ONE WHO ORDERS TO HOLD IT.

WRITING IS INVENTED AND ZERO CREATED.

CALENDARIC COUNT DEVELOPS AND PERFECTS ITSELF AND THE FIRST STONE-ARCHITECTURE APEARS. **THE DEPARTURE OF THE MAYA CULTURE !**

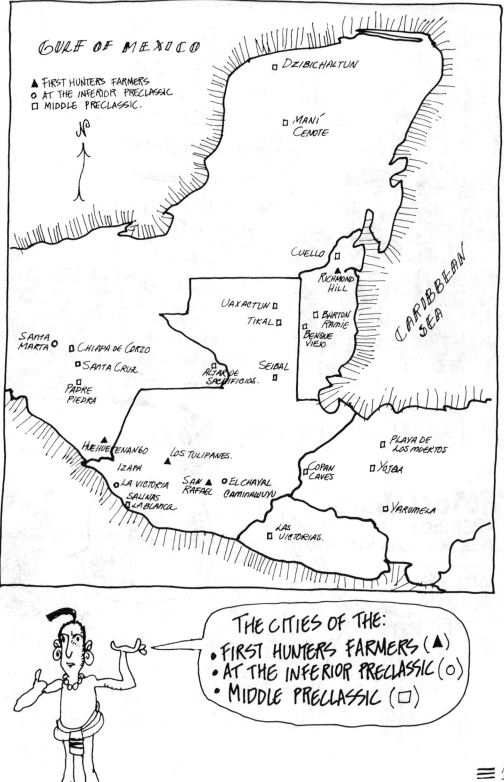

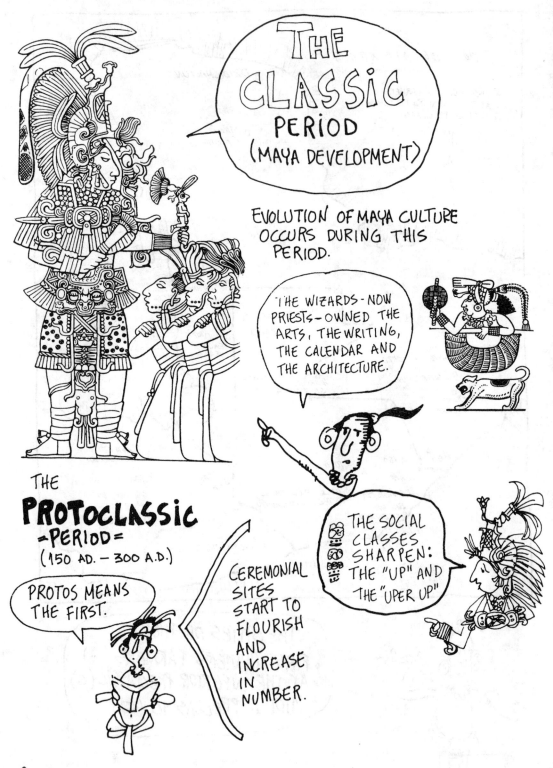

THE CLASSIC PERIOD
(MAYA DEVELOPMENT)

EVOLUTION OF MAYA CULTURE OCCURS DURING THIS PERIOD.

THE WIZARDS - NOW PRIESTS - OWNED THE ARTS, THE WRITING, THE CALENDAR AND THE ARCHITECTURE.

THE SOCIAL CLASSES SHARPEN: THE "UP" AND THE "UPER UP"

THE PROTOCLASSIC =PERIOD=
(150 AD. — 300 A.D.)

PROTOS MEANS THE FIRST.

CEREMONIAL SITES START TO FLOURISH AND INCREASE IN NUMBER.

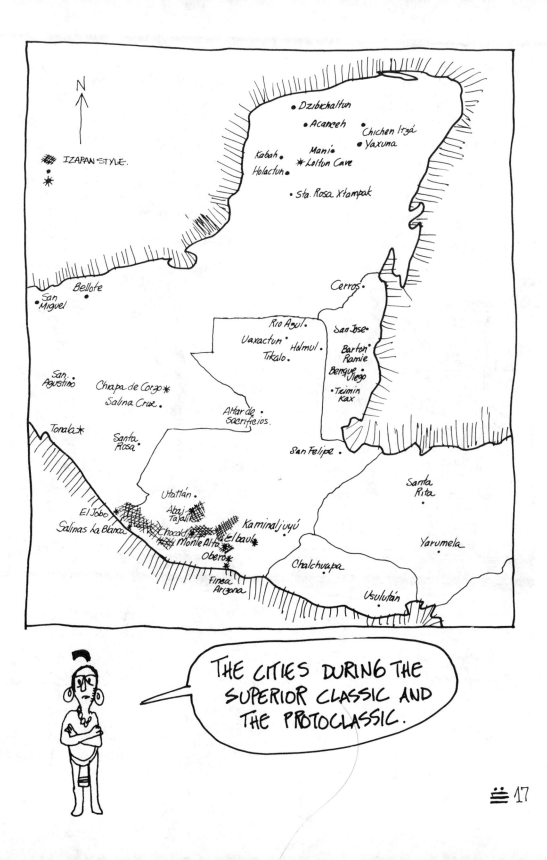

THE CITIES DURING THE SUPERIOR CLASSIC AND THE PROTOCLASSIC.

17

THE EARLY CLASSIC PERIOD

(300 AD. — 600 AD.)

IN THIS PERIOD THE MAYA CULTURE GET'S TO THE TOP.

SOCIETY ENLARGES AND MAGNIFIES THANKS TO SEVERAL ACHIEVEMENTS:

IT IS BELIVED THAT CHANNELS AND TERRACES THAT FACILITATES IRRIGATION RESULTS IN AGRICULTURAL ADVAN--CEMENT, MONEY FLOWS, ENHANCED BY THE GROWING COMMERCIAL EXCHANGE. IMPROVEMENTS ARE MADE IN ARCHITECTURE, MATHEMATICS, ASTRONOMY AND WRITING.

WHAT IS CULTURE FOR?

For us

THE RULING CLASS USED THIS PROGRES IN ITS OWN BENEFIT, GROWING ITS POWER OVER THE PEOPLE.

WHAT REALLY HAPPENED WAS THE CONVERSION OF A GOVERMENT IN A TEOCRACY (GOBERMENT BY PRIESTS) MANTEINED BY THE PEOPLES TAXES AND TRIBUTES

$

THE LATE CLASSIC
(600 TO 900 AD.

BY THIS YEARS THE MAYA CULTURE EXCELS. POPULATION GROW AND NEW LANDS COME UNDER CONTROL.

AND WE PAY THE BILL!

SWEAR IT!

CEREMONIAL SITES START TO FLOURISH AND INCREASE IN NUMBER

THIS SHOWS THE IMPORTANCE OF RELIGIOUS BELIEFS AMONG THE MAYA AS AN INSTRUMENT OF POWER OF THE UPER CLASES.

ROYALTY, SHID!

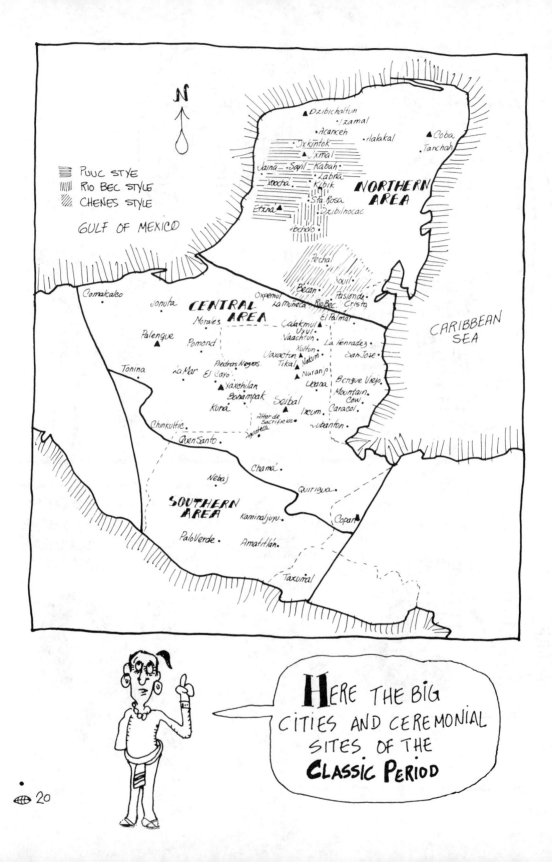

N

PUUC STYE
RIO BEC STYLE
CHENES STYLE

GULF OF MEXICO

▲Dzibichaltun
•Izamal
•Acanceh
•Ilalakal
▲Ikkintok
▲Uxmal
Jaina• •Sayil •Kabah
Xocha• •Labna
•Kabik
•Sta Rosa
Etzna ▲ •Dzibilnocac
•Ixchilo

NORTHERN
AREA

▲Coba
▲Tanchah

Pechal

•Oxil
Bécan • Hasiende
Oxpemul •Rio Bec. •Crista
La Muneca•
El Palmar

Comalcalco•
•Jonuta
CENTRAL
AREA
Morales•
•Calakmul
•Uxul
•Vaachtun
Palenque ▲ •Pomond
•La Henradez
Yaxactun• Xultun
Tikal• Natum•
▲ •SanJose
•Naranjo
Tonina• La Mar• El Cayo Piedras Negros• •Utana •Benque Viejo
▲Yaxchilan Mountain
Bonampak Cow
Kuna• Seibal •Caracol
•Ixcun
•Altar de •Lubanton
Sacrificios•
Chinkultic• Joptatea•

CARIBBEAN
SEA

QvenSanto•

•Chama

•Nebaj
SOUTHERN
AREA
•Kaminaljuyu
•Quirigua
•Copan

PaloVerde• •Amatitlan

•Taxumal

HERE THE BIG
CITIES AND CEREMONIAL
SITES OF THE
CLASSIC PERIOD

🌐 20

THE **POST-CLASSIC** PERIOD

LET'S START WITH THE **EARLY POST-CLASSIC**, LASTING FROM (1000 AD TO 1250 AD.)

THE TOLTECS CAME AND A "MAYA-TOLTEC" CULTURE BEGAN

DURING THIS PERIOD, **COMERCIAL** ACTIVITIES GET **STRONGER** PARTICULARY INVOLVING THE CENTER OF MEXICO AND CENTRAL AMERICA.

FROM SOME TO EXPORT, OTHERS HAD THEIR NECKS BROKEN.

IN ORDER TO SUPPLY THE DEMAND OF EXTERNAL MARKETS, EXPLOITATION OF THE PEOPLE INCREASES. PRODUCTION OF SALT, HONEY, COPAL AND COTTON NOTICEABLY AUGMENTED.

ALL FOR ONE AND ONE FOR ME!

MERCHANTS, ARISTOCRACY AND PRIESTHOOD ORGANIZED A COMMON FRONT WHILE

MiLiTARY POWER GUARANTEED PRODUCTION.

GOOD GRIEF!

... 23

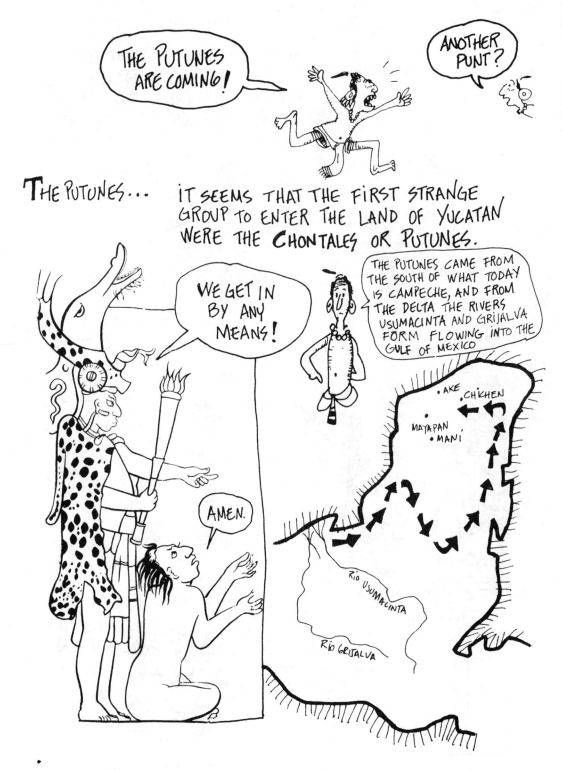

THE PUTUNES ARE COMING!

ANOTHER PUNT?

THE PUTUNES...

IT SEEMS THAT THE FIRST STRANGE GROUP TO ENTER THE LAND OF YUCATAN WERE THE CHONTALES OR PUTUNES.

THE PUTUNES CAME FROM THE SOUTH OF WHAT TODAY IS CAMPECHE, AND FROM THE DELTA THE RIVERS USUMACINTA AND GRIJALVA FORM FLOWING INTO THE GULF OF MEXICO

WE GET IN BY ANY MEANS!

AMEN.

AKE
CHICHEN
MAYAPAN
MANI

RÍO USUMACINTA

RÍO GRIJALVA

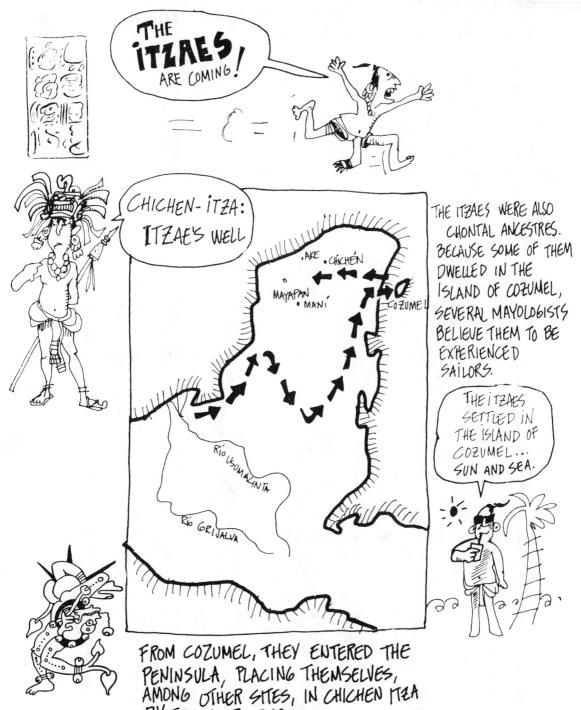

THE ITZAES ARE COMING!

CHICHEN-ITZA: ITZAE'S WELL

THE ITZAES WERE ALSO CHONTAL ANCESTRES. BECAUSE SOME OF THEM DWELLED IN THE ISLAND OF COZUMEL, SEVERAL MAYOLOGISTS BELIEVE THEM TO BE EXPERIENCED SAILORS.

THE ITZAES SETTLED IN THE ISLAND OF COZUMEL... SUN AND SEA.

FROM COZUMEL, THEY ENTERED THE PENINSULA, PLACING THEMSELVES, AMONG OTHER SITES, IN CHICHEN ITZA BY THE YEAR 918 AD.

THIS GROUP ROULED A VAST REGION, MANTAINING COMMERCIAL RELATIONS WITH WHAT TODAY ARE THE MEXICAN STATES OF TABASCO AND CAMPECHE.

ITWAS PRECISELY BY TABASCO AND CAMPECHE WHERE A NEW GROUP SPEAKING NAHUATL AND HEAVILY INFLUENCED BY THE CULTURE OF TULA (TOLTEC) ARRIVED TO CHICHEN ITZA IN THE YEAR 970 AD.

THIS IS THE WAY KUKUL CAN (FEATHERED SERPENT CAME TO YUCATAN)

AT CHICHEN ITZA THEY BUILT THE TEMPLE OF WARRIORS, THE CASTLE AND THE BALL FIELD.

KUKULCAN NEGOTIATED WITH SEVERAL CHIEFS OF THE SORROUNDINGS, TO CONVINCE THEM TO ERECT A NEW CITY WHERE EVERYTHING THAT IS GOOD WOULD SPRING.

GOOD GOVERMENT COMMERCE, ARTS.

THE CITY KUKULKAN FOUNDED WAS MAYAPAN (THE "FLAG OF THE MAYA") WERE EVERYBODY LIVED HAPPILY EVER AFTER IN HARMONY WITH ALL THE PETTY KINGS.

AFTER THAT KUKULKAN WENT BACK TO TULA, HIS ORIGINAL DEPARTURE'S SITE

MR. KUKULKAN WAS SUCH A NICE GUY, WE TOOK HIM FOR A GOD

BY GOD!

THE **XIUES** ARE COMING!

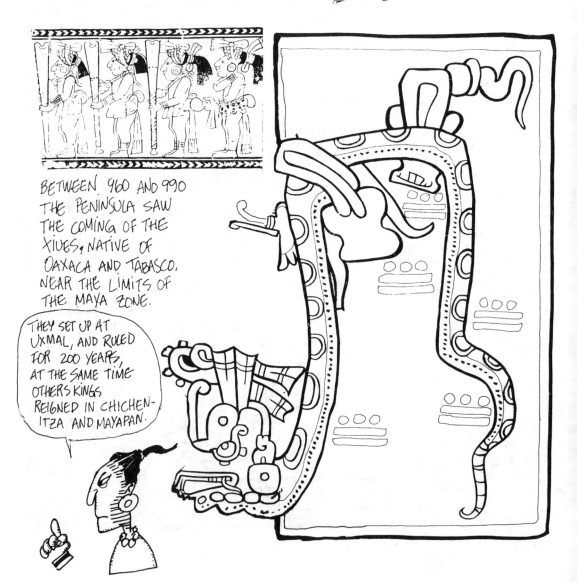

BETWEEN 960 AND 990 THE PENINSULA SAW THE COMING OF THE XIUES, NATIVE OF OAXACA AND TABASCO, NEAR THE LIMITS OF THE MAYA ZONE.

THEY SET UP AT UXMAL, AND RULED FOR 200 YEARS, AT THE SAME TIME OTHERS KINGS REIGNED IN CHICHEN-ITZA AND MAYAPAN.

THE LATE POST-CLASSIC PERIOD (1250 - 1524 / 1542 AD.)

THIS PERIOD MARKS THE SOCIOECO-NOMIC, POLITICAL, AND CULTURAL DESINTE-GRATION OF THE MAYA.

MAYAPAN BECOMES THE RULER OVER THE REST OF **Y**UCATAN KINGDOMS

AND THE COMUNITARY LAND?

THEY PASSED TO THE HANDS OF WARRIORS AND MERCHANTS.

OPRESSED... WHO'S OPRESSED?

SOCIAL CONTRADICTIONS SURGE AND A POPULAR REBELION FINISHES THE POWER OF **COCOM**, A FAMILY THAT GOVERNED AT MAYAPAN.

THIS CITY IS ERRADICATED (PUT TO SHAMBLES) THE CACIQUE. TYPE OF RULING APPEAR... LITTLE INDEPENDENT STATES, OR CITY-STATES AND THEIR SMALL POWERS WERE WHAT THE SPANIARDS FOUND.

DEATH TO THE UNFAITHFUL!

AFTER THE FALL OF MAYAPAN THE MAYA EMPIRE FRACTIONED IN "CACICAZGOS", FOLLOWED BY EIGTHY YEARS OF POLITICAL FAILURE. THE MAYA WERE IN THE ROAD OF HELL WHEN THEY CAME... THE BEARDED ONES, THE REPRESENTATIVES OF THE OLD WORLD... THE **SPANIARDS**, BRINGING THE SWORD, THE CROSS AND THE INEVITABLE NEW DESEASES.

NONTHELESS, MAYAPAN BECAUSE OF THE FAMOUS "LIGA" (THE ALLIANCE OF MAYAPAN), DESERVES A HISTORIC CAPSULE...

LONG LIVE SPAIN, YOU BASTARDS!

COMING NEXT!

THE MAYAPAN ALLIANCE

COMMON MARKET AND NO BELIGERANCE PACT.

THE MAYAPAN ALLIANCE OR LEAGUE WAS COMPOSED BY UXMAL, CHICHEN ITZA AND MAYAPAN, AMONG OTHER CITY STATES OF THE REGION.

IT WAS A HAPPY ERA, LASTING 200 YEARS.

IN CHICHEN, THE TOLTEC-MAYA ART DEVELOPED.

THE GOOD TIMES WERE TO MUCH TO BE TRUE. "OFFICIAL HISTORY" CONSIDERS THE KIDNNAPPING OF A MAYAPAN CHIEF'S BRIDE AS THE REASON OF THE WAR...

A FENOMENAL QUARREL BEGAN. MAYAPAN BATLED AGAINST THE ITZAES, BEATING THEM... AND VICEVERSA. THE CITY OF MAYAPAN FELL UNDER THE ITZAES' ATTACK.

MAYAPAN, RA, RA, RA!

LET'S GET SOME NAHUATL MERCENARY SOLDIERS AND IN FINISHING WITH THE ITZAES, I SHARE WITH THEM THE SPOILS OF WAR.

← MAYAPAN CACIQUE ASHAMED BY ITZAES' VICTORY.

AND THAT'S THE WAY IT WAS: MAYAPAN CONQUERED THE WHOLE YUCATAN IMPOSING A CENTRAL GOVERMENT.

AS TIME WENT BY, THE GOVERMENT BECAME RUTHLESS AND DESPOTIC.

ARTS WERE DENIED, BUT SEVERAL PRO- GRESSES APPEAR: BOW AND ARROWS, AS USEFUL FOR GAME AS FOR THE WAR.

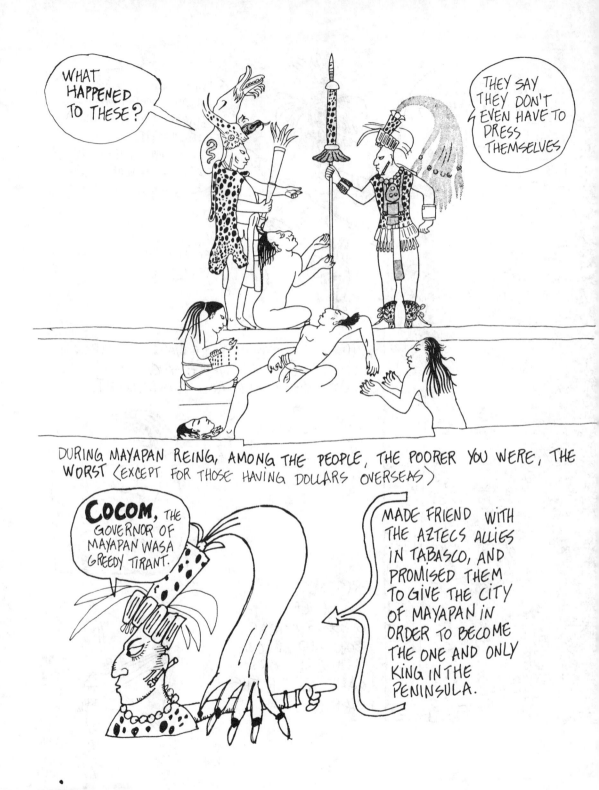

DURING MAYAPAN REING, AMONG THE PEOPLE, THE POORER YOU WERE, THE WORST (EXCEPT FOR THOSE HAVING DOLLARS OVERSEAS)

COCOM, THE GOVERNOR OF MAYAPAN WAS A GREEDY TIRANT.

MADE FRIEND WITH THE AZTECS ALLIES IN TABASCO, AND PROMISED THEM TO GIVE THE CITY OF MAYAPAN IN ORDER TO BECOME THE ONE AND ONLY KING IN THE PENINSULA.

COCOM BROUGHT THE MEXICAS OR NAHUATLS TO MAYAPAN AND WITH THEIR HELP STARTED A REGIMEN OF OPRESION.

COCOM HAS THE DUBIOUS HONOR OF BEING THE FIRST MAYA WHO ENSLAVED MEN BY HIMSELF.

THE OTHER MAYAPAN CHIEFS SWALOWED SHIT AND HAD TO OBEY COCOM.

THINGS WERE THERE TO STAY. A LITTLE COCOM FOLLOWED THE FIRST COCOM AND USED THE SAME TACTICS.

COCOM'S HEIRS SEEMED TO BE WORST THAN THE ORIGINAL ONE. TIRANNY, SLAVERY, AND OPRESSION WERE THE DAILY RATION FOR ALL.

...UNTILL INTRIGUE MADE ITS ENTRANCE

BZZZ BZZZ

THE XIUES, TAUGHT BY THE MEXICAS THE USE OF BOW AND ARROWS, UNITED UNDER THE RULE OF TUTUL-XIU, AN OLD WARRIOR.

DEATH TO THE COCOMES!

THE XIUES KILLED COCOM AND TOOK HIS PROPERTIES

THE END OF MAYAPAN SIGNAL THE LAST "CEREMONIAL" CIVILIZATION IN CENTRAL AMERICA.

THE GENERALITIES

HERE WE TELL HOW THE
MAYA BEHAVED IN:

- SOCIETY
- POLITICS
- RELIGION
- ART
- SCIENCE
- SOCIAL HABITS
- COMMERCE
- INDUSTRY
- AGRICULTURE

... AND SEVERAL ETCETERAS.

SOCIETY

NOBILITY

TWO GROUPS COMPOSED THE ARISTOCRACY:
1) THE **AHKINOOB** AND
2) THE **ALMEHENOOB**.

THE AHKINOOB

WAS THE GROUP FORMED BY THE **PRIESTHOOD**, THEY WERE ALSO CALLED "THOSE OF THE SUN"

DID THEY SHINE?

THE ALMEHENOOB

WERE ALSO CALLED THE **MASTERS**, THEY WERE SAID TO HAVE MOTHER AND FATHER

ALTHOUGH THEY BEHAVED IN A MOTHERLESS MANNER.

PRICES HIKES IN CORN AND HONEY IS THE ONLY THING THAT INTERESTS ME.

THE MERCHANTS

THEY WERE THE INTERMEDIATE CLASS, BUT ASPIRING TO BELONG TO THE NOBILITY.

AT THE END. THE POPULATION, THE COMMON PEOPLE DIVIDED IN:

1) THE **AH CHEMBAL UINICOOB**
2) THE **YALBA UINICOOB** AND
3) THE **PPENCATOOB**

TO MUCH "OOB", BUT NOT MUCH FOOD

THEY LIVE BLAIMING US!

1) **THE AH CHEMBAL UINICOOB**

THEY WERE THE "INFERIOR" THE "VULGAR" MEN.

VULGAR? YOUR MOTHER!

2) **THE YALBA UINICOOB**

THEY WERE AS POOR AS THE AH CHEMBAL UINICOOB THEY WERE CONSIDERED "SMALL" OR PLEBEIANS.

3) **THE PPENCATOOB**

THEY WERE THE LOW-LOW ONES: THE SLAVES.

ANYONE COULD BE ENSLAVED BY ANY OF THESE REASONS

A) FOR BEING BORN IN SLAVERY

B) WHEN TAKEN PRISIONER IN A WAR.

C) FOR BURGLARY

D) BECAUSE SOME ONE BOUGHT YOU

E) BY BEING AN ORPHAN.

THE (DIRTY) POLITICS

FORGIVE THE REDUNDANCE, BUT NOBILITY AND GOVERMENT WAS THE SAME. THINGS WERE MORE OR LESS LIKE THIS:

ON YOUR KNEES, PLEASE.

STEPPING ON THE WHOLE NATION WAS THE **HALACH UINIC** (MEANING "TRUE MAN", "KING", "MONARCH", "SUPER MASTER") ALSO NAMED **AHAU,** WHO HAD CIVIL AND RELIGIOUS FUNCTIONS.

HIS WORD WAS THE LAST IN EXTERNAL AND INTERNAL POLITICS.

THE OFFICE WAS HEREDITARY, HIS OLDEST SON RECEIVING THE POWER, BUT NOT HAVING A FIRST SON AT THE TIME OF DEATH, THE SCEPTER WENT TO HIS OLDER BROTHER.

SECOND IN THE HIERARCHY WERE THE **AH CUCH CAB**, "THE ONES IN THE COUNCIL", 2 OR 3 OF THEM, EACH ONE INFUENCING THE GOVERMENTAL DESITIONS. THEIR APPROVAL WAS INDISPENSABLE FOR ANY GOVERMENTAL DECITIONS.

A BRIBE A DAY KEEPS THE COUNCIL AWAY.

BELOW THEM WERE THE **BATABOOB**, LESSER CHIEFS WITH CIVIL AND RELIGIOUS FUNCTIONS. EACH BATAB HAD HIS OWN SOLDIERS (THEY WERE, BESIDES, SOLDIERS), BUT DURING WAR TIMES THEY ALL SERVED A SUPREME MILITARY CHIEF: THE **NACOM.**

THEY WERE FAMILY OF THE **HALACH UINIC** THERE WAS A REAL NEPOTISM

THE BATABOOB CHAIRED THE COUNCIL, KEPT THE MAINTE-NANCE AND ORDER OF THE HOUSES AND TOWN CONSTRUCTIONS, AND SAW TO IT THAT PEOPLE PAID TRIBUTES TO THE HALACH HUINIC.

BELOW THEM CAME THE **AH KULELOOB,** SORT OF ATTORNEYS WHO EXECUTED THE BATABOOB'S ORDERS, AND ACOMPAINIED THEM EVERYWERE THEY WENT. THEY WERE NO MORE THAN THREE.

WHAT MY **BATAB** SAYS IS WELL SAID.

THEN CAME THE **AH HOLPOPOOB** (THOSE WHO SAT AT THE HONOR PLACE, SORT OF A CHAIRMAN). IT IS TOLD THAT THEY HELPED THE GOVERNORS AND CARED ON THE POPOLNA, THE HOUSE WERE MEN GATHERED TO DEAL PUBLIC AFFAIRES AND TO LEARN THE RITUAL DANCES.

THE **AH HOLPOP** WAS THE MAN SINGER, IN CHARGE OF DANCES AN MUSICAL INSTRU--MENTS IN EVERY TOWN.

THE LAW!

LAST WERE THE **TUPILES,** SORT OF POLICEMEN WHO EXECUTED THE SUPERIOR ORDERS AND GOT THE JOB DONE.

RELIGION

... THE FAMOUS OPIUM ...

MAYA RELIGION MEANS **POLITEISM** AT IT'S BEST.

WE HAD GODS EVEN TO GO TO THE BATHROOM

SOME GODS GET AWAY VERY WELL WITH THE PEOPLE, OTHERS...

SEEMED TO ENJOY WITH OUR SUFFERINGS.

AND OF COURSE, OTHERS WERE AMBIVALENT GODS.

GODS REPRESENTING NATURAL FORCES (WATER, RAIN, WIND) WERE HONORED WITH PARTICULAR DEVOTION.

DO I WANT RAIN? I PRAY TO CHAAC AND THAT'S ALL.

THE BELIEFS

'TILL I SEE I'LL BELIEVE

WE BELIEVED, THANK GOD, IN SOUL'S INMORTALITY AND FUTURE LIFE TOO -AMEN-

MAYA BELIEVED THAT PRIESTS, DEAD IN BATTLE, WOMEN THAT DIED GIVING BIRTH, AND THE SACRIFICED TO THE GODS, WENT DIRECTLY TO HEAVEN. (A FIVE STARS ONE).

AT THE UPPER HEAVEN, THERE WAS A GIANT CEIBA (SORT OF THE FIRST TREE OF THE WORLD), ITS SHADOW GAVE TO THE WARMED SOULS A CELESTIAL REST.

YOU'VE GOT TO SEE HOW ONE SWEATS IN THIS CLIMATE TO GO TO HEAVEN

THE MITNAL -SORT OF HELL- THRIVE UNDER MANAGEMENT OF AH PUCH, OF WHOM I PREFER TO KEEP SILENCE.

RELiGiOUS FESTiViTIES AND RITES

THE MAYA BELIVED BLINDLY THAT THE PRIESTS KNEW IN EVERY SINGLE DETAIL, WHAT THE GODS WANTED AND DISAGREED. AND WHAT HAPPENED WHEN PRIESTS WENT WRONG?

IT WAS BECAUSE GODS WERE ANGRY.

FOR THE MAYA, EXISTENCE WAS TIED TO TIME, THE LATTER IN-FLUENCING DIRECTLY THE FATE (DESTINY)

EVERY FESTIVITY STARTED WITH FASTINGS, EXORCISMS AND TEMPERANCE, PARTICULARY THE NEW YEARS CELEBRATION THE FIRST DAY OF THE MONTH POP.

←TACO

PRIEST FASTENED THE MOST, IN ORDER TO IMPRESS THE PEOPLE.

EVERY HOUSE WAS CLEAN, HOME IMPLEMENTS AND ALL TRASH THROWN OUT OF TOWN.

THE MAYA COSMOGONY

THE MAYAS SAW THE WORD AS A CUBE, THE HEAVENS ABOVE AND THE HELL BELOW.

THEY HAD 13 HEAVENS PLACED ONE OVER THE OTHER. IN EACH SLICE OF THE SANDWICH A SUPE- RIOR WORLD-GOD REIGNED. THESE GODS WERE CALLED OXLAHUNTIKU.

LOOKING DOWN, THEY HAD ANOTHER NINE SLICES OF THE HELL SANDWICH, EVERY ONE WITH ITS OWN GOD. THESE GODS WERE NAMED BOLONTIKU.

THE FIRST SLICE OF THE 13 SUPERIOR WORLDS WAS THE EARTH.

THE MITNAL, THE LOWEST INFRA-WORLD, THE PLACE OF AH PUCH, THE GOD OF DEATH (OF WHOM I PREFER NOT TO TALK)

← AH PUCH: DON'T BE RIDICULOUS?

THE **BACABES** WERE AT THE FOURTH EXTREMITIES OF THE WORLD.

WE WERE HOLDING IT!

WORLD

ZAC
NORTH
(YELLOW)

EK
WEST
(BLACK)

YAX
CENTER
(GREEN)

CHAC
EAST
(RED)

KAN
SOUTH
(YELLOW)

EACH ONE HAD A COLOR AND THIS COLOR NAMED THE OCCUPANT BACAB.

ACORDING THE **POPOL VUH**, (THE MAYA BIBLE) AT THE BEGINNING IT WAS THE SEA AND THE SKY. SINCE THIS WAS SO BOREDOM THE CREATOR PUT HIMSELF TO WORK, INVENTING RIVERS, TREES AND ANIMALS.

AND THEN, CHAC CREATED MEN TO BE ADORED AND TO RECIEVE THEIR GRATITUDE.

THE FIRST GOD-MADE MAN WAS A FAILURE: HE WAS MADE OUT OF CLAY

WITH A LITTLE BIT OF SHIT, OF COURSE

THE SECOND INPROVED A LITTLE: IT WAS MADE OUT OF WOOD, BUT HE DIDN'T KNOW HOW TO WORSHIP THE GODS, A SMALL DEFECTS THAT GODS DIDN'T LIKE. SO THEY SENT THAT ROTTED EVERY MAN ON THE SURFACE OF THE EARTH... AND HAVING NO NOAH. HOW COULD THESE WOODEN MEN BE SAVED?

THESE WOODEN MEN REPRODUCED THEMSELVES. DON'T ASK ME HOW.

DINNER IS READY!

AN THEN IT OCCURRED TO THEM THAT **CORN-MADE** MEN WOULD BE BETTER OF. EXACTLY: C-O-R-N.

FLESH WAS MADE OF YELLOW CORN AND WHITE CORN.

THE FIRST FOUR MEN CREATED (OR VICTIMS AS YOU WISH) WERE:

- **BALAM-QUITZÉ**
- **BALAM-ACAB**
- **MAHUCUTAH**
- **IQUÍ-BALAM**

THE CREATOR WAS GENTLE ENOUGH TO PROVIDE EVERY ONE WITH A WIFE.

FROM THERE ON IT WAS A MATTER OF TIME THE UPSURGE OF TRIBES, TOWNS AND CITIES. AND THEIR DECENDENCE POPULATED THE WORLD.

THE MAYA REVERED A CREATOR GOD "THE TOUGH GUY" CALLED **HUNAB-KU**

AND AFTER HIM A LONG LIST OF GODS: FOR THE RAIN, FOR THE HURRICANE, FOR THE DROUGHT, ETC.

TO THEM THE MAYA ATRIBUTED CONTRADIC--TORY ORIGINS AND QUALITIES.

THIS IS THE GOD'S HIERARCHY.

- GODS OF THE SKY
- GODS OF THE ELEMENTS
- PATRON GODS
- UNDERGROUND GODS (OR GODS OF THE INFRAWORLD)
- WAR GODS
- TIME AND NUMBER GODS

THE SKY GODS

KIN (THE SUN) PATRONIZED MUSIC, POETRY AND HUNTING.

UH (THE MOON) PATRONIZED CORN, KNIT AND WEAVING, CROPS AND CHILDBRITH.

XAMAN EK ≈ ⇨
(THE GOD OF THE NORTH STAR) PATRON OF TRAVELERS AND MERCHANTS.

NOH EK THE PLANET VENUS.
(EK MEANS "STAR" IN MAYA)

GODS OF THE ELEMENTS

AS THE CHAIRMAN OF THE MAYA PANTHEON IS ITZAMNA, A GOOD GOD, FRIEND OF THE HUMANS MASTER OF THE SKY, THE DAY AND THE NIGHT.

ITZAMNÁ
(THE SON OF HUNAB--KU THE CREATOR)

FIRST PLACE IN CELESTIAL BUROCRACY

ITZAMNA WAS THE FIRST PRIEST, THE INVENTOR OF WRITING AND BOOKS, HE WAS INVOCKED TO PREVENT PUBLIC DISGRACES.

ITZAMNA WAS THE PATRON OF THE **AHAU** DAY, THE PRINCIPAL DAY OF THE 20 EACH MONTH HAD

HE NAMED THE DIFFERENT YUCATAN REGIONS.

CHAAC

CHAAC IS RAIN'S GOD AND EVERYTHING RELATED TO IT.

LIGHTNING, RAY, THUNDER; AS AN AGRICULTURAL PATRON, CHAAC IS A RELATIVE OF ALL GODS IN CONNECTION TO IT.

CHAAC WAS NOT A ONE AND ONLY GOD, HE WAS FOUR DIFFERENTS GODS AND A TRULY ONE.

CHAAC WAS THE FOUR CARDINAL POINTS, EACH ONE WITH ITS OWN COLOR.

A) CHAAC XIB CHAAC
THE RED MAN, OR EAST CHAAC.

B) SAC XIB CHAAC
OR WITHE MAN, THE NORTH CHAAC.

C) EK XIB CHAAC
OR BLACK MAN, THE WEST CHAAC.

D) KAN XIB CHAAC
OR YELLOW MAN, THE SOUTH CHAAC.

BE CAREFUL CHAAC!

BESIDES CHAAC, THERE WERE THE "CHAQUES" FOR MINISTERS OR HELPERS. THE OLD CHAAC DELEGATED HIS FUNCTIONS ON.

NO MINIMUM SALARY, NO RAISES NO INFLATION COMPENSATION.

THE CHAQUES CARRIED WITH THEM PUMPKINS, FILLED WITH WATER, BAGS FULL OF WIND AND A DRUM.

WHILE WORKING THE CHAQUES STROKE THE GREAT PUMPKIN LETTING THE WATER DROP: THAT WAS THE RAIN.

WHEN THE BAGS WERE OPENED, THE WIND BLOWED, THUNDER WAS A MATTER OF DRUMMING.

ALONG WITH THESE EXISTED OTHER FOUR BROTHERS, THE **BACABES**

THEY TOOK THE CHARGE OF PROTECTING HUMAN KIND, BECAUSE THEY HELD THE SKY AND THE HEAVEN AT THE FOUR CARDINAL POINTS TO PREVENT THE WATER FROM SPILLING OVER THE EARTH.

ACCORDING TO THE YEAR, THE BACABES BROUGHT GOOD OR BAD FORTUNE

THE PATRON GODS

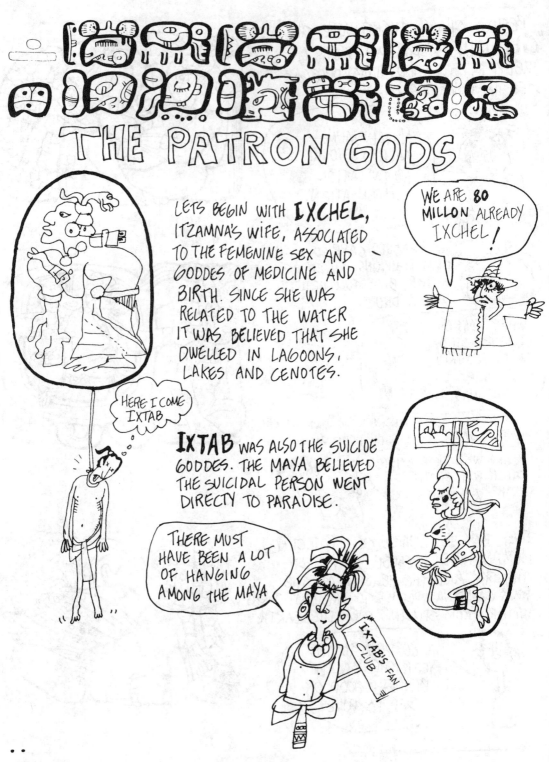

LETS BEGIN WITH **IXCHEL**, ITZAMNA'S WIFE, ASSOCIATED TO THE FEMENINE SEX AND GODDES OF MEDICINE AND BIRTH. SINCE SHE WAS RELATED TO THE WATER IT WAS BELIEVED THAT SHE DWELLED IN LAGOONS, LAKES AND CENOTES.

WE ARE **80** MILLON ALREADY IXCHEL!

HERE I COME IXTAB

IXTAB WAS ALSO THE SUICIDE GODDES. THE MAYA BELIEVED THE SUICIDAL PERSON WENT DIRECTY TO PARADISE.

THERE MUST HAVE BEEN A LOT OF HANGING AMONG THE MAYA

IXTAB'S FAN CLUB

EK CHUAH WAS
THE GOD OF THE DEALERS, AND THE PATRON OF CACAO, BUT HE REMAINED A "DOUBLE STANDARD GOD"

WHEN IN A GOOD MOOD, HE PROTECTS THE MERCHANTS

WHEN IN A BAD MOOD HE'S ASSOCIATED TO WAR

CHUAH-CHUAH SEND MONEY CHUAH-CHUAH!

* MERCHANTS IN CRISIS TIME.

HERE COMES THE MASTER OF THE FIELDS, THE AGRICULTURE AND THE CORN

YUM KAX
(THE LETTER "X" IN MAYA SOUNDS APROXIMATELY LIKE "SH" IN ENGLISH)

YUM KAX WAS THE PATRON OF FARMING AND, THE SAME AS CORN, HAD MANY ENEMIES, HIS FATE WAS TIED TO THE GODS OF RAIN, THE DROUGHT, THE WIND, THE STARVATION AND DEATH.

KAX-KAX YUM-KAX

LAST BUT NO LEAST THE **MUCEMCABOOB**, GOD BEE'S SOVEREINGS OF THE FOREST. AND

BZZZZ-z-z-z

THE **MAMES**, GODS OF EVILNESS THAT APPEAR ONLY DURING FAMINE AND BAD TIMES.

LET'S BEAT IT!

THE UNDERGROUND GODS

FROM THE INFRAWORLD

HERE COMES, THE ONE, THE ONLY, Mr. **AH PUCH** GENERAL MANAGER OF HELL INC.

WHOM I DIDN'T WANT TO TALK ABOUT!

AH PUCH
(GOD OF THE DEATH)

HE'S THE BAD GUY, ASSOCIATED TO WAR AND HUMAN SACRIFICES. HIS FRIENDS: THE DOG, THE MOÁN BIRD AND THE OWL, ALL BAD LUCK ANIMALS.
THE **JAGUAR** GOD AND THE **BOLONTIKU**, OR NINE MASTERS OF THE NIGHT, COMPLETED THE INFERNAL KINGDOME.

THE WAR GODS

¡CHUC!

THESE ARE THE COMPANIONS OF AH PUCH WHEN HE PLAY'S GAMES.

AS FAR AS THINGS GO, THEY MUST BE RUNNING THE SHOW TODAY.

THE DAYS, THE MONTHS, AND THE NUMBERS ONE TO THIRTEEN WERE ALSO GODS. THEY WERE THE GODS OF TIME AND NUMBERS.

I L♥VE THE NINE WHEN IT COME'S WITH SIX ZEROES.

THIS CHAPTER COULD NOT END WITHOUT MENTIONING **KUKULCAN**, MAN CREATED GOD, NAMER OF ALL PLACES, DISTRIBUITOR OF THE LAND (NO AGRARIAN REFORM NEEDED) AND WRITING INUENTOR.

FIRST

SECOND   THIRD

FOURTH   FIFTH   SIXTH

SEVENTH   EIGHT   NINTH

HIEROGLYFS OF THE NINE NAMES OF TRUCULENT REGION DEITIES.

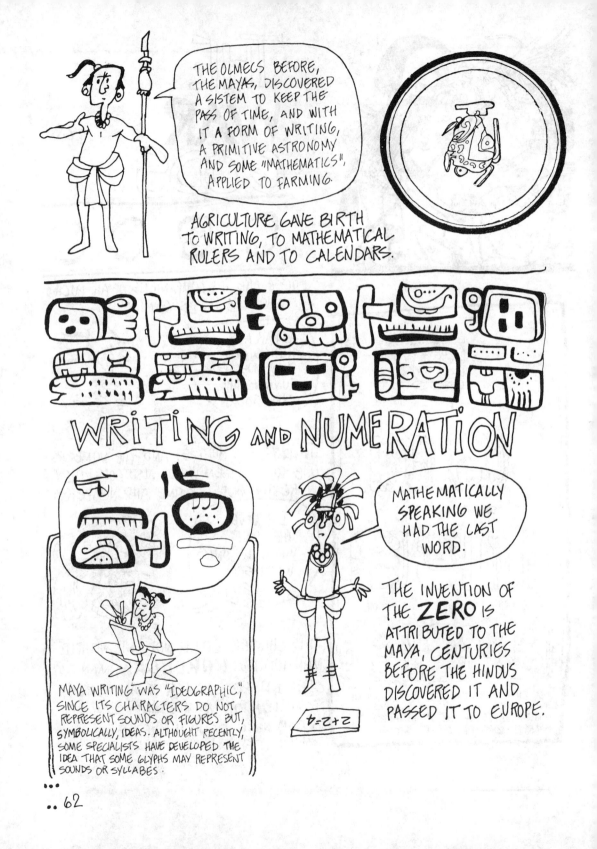

THE OLMECS BEFORE, THE MAYAS, DISCOVERED A SISTEM TO KEEP THE PASS OF TIME, AND WITH IT A FORM OF WRITING, A PRIMITIVE ASTRONOMY AND SOME "MATHEMATICS", APPLIED TO FARMING.

AGRICULTURE GAVE BIRTH TO WRITING, TO MATHEMATICAL RULERS AND TO CALENDARS.

WRITING AND NUMERATION

MATHEMATICALLY SPEAKING WE HAD THE LAST WORD.

MAYA WRITING WAS "IDEOGRAPHIC", SINCE ITS CHARACTERS DO NOT REPRESENT SOUNDS OR FIGURES BUT, SYMBOLICALLY, IDEAS. ALTHOUGHT RECENTLY, SOME SPECIALISTS HAVE DEVELOPED THE IDEA THAT SOME GLYPHS MAY REPRESENT SOUNDS OR SYLLABES.

THE INVENTION OF THE **ZERO** IS ATTRIBUTED TO THE MAYA, CENTURIES BEFORE THE HINDUS DISCOVERED IT AND PASSED IT TO EUROPE.

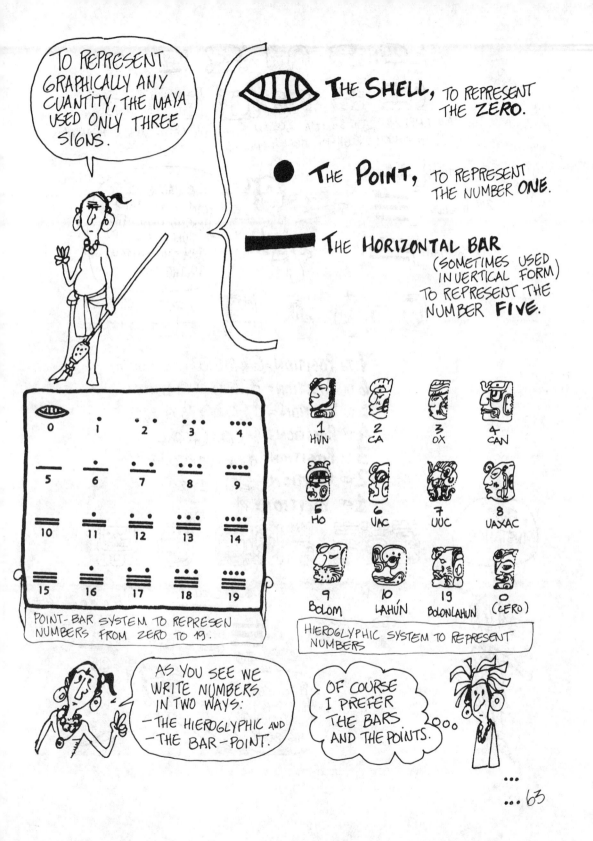

TO REPRESENT GRAPHICALLY ANY CUANTITY, THE MAYA USED ONLY THREE SIGNS.

THE SHELL, TO REPRESENT THE ZERO.

THE POINT, TO REPRESENT THE NUMBER ONE.

THE HORIZONTAL BAR (SOMETIMES USED IN VERTICAL FORM) TO REPRESENT THE NUMBER FIVE.

0	1	2	3	4
5	6	7	8	9
10	11	12	13	14
15	16	17	18	19

POINT-BAR SYSTEM TO REPRESEN NUMBERS FROM ZERO TO 19.

1 HUN	2 CA	3 OX	4 CAN
5 HO	6 UAC	7 UUC	8 UAXAC
9 BOLOM	10 LAHÚN	19 BOLONLAHUN	0 (CERO)

HIEROGLYPHIC SYSTEM TO REPRESENT NUMBERS

AS YOU SEE WE WRITE NUMBERS IN TWO WAYS:
- THE HIEROGLYPHIC AND
- THE BAR-POINT.

OF COURSE I PREFER THE BARS AND THE POINTS.

THE MAYA EMPLOYED A VIGESIMAL SYSTEM (FROM THE LATIN WORLD MEANING TWENTY) IN WHICH ONE UNITY REALLY MEANS TWENTY UNITS.

3RD POSITION

2ND POSITION

1ST POSITION

THE VALUE OF POINTS AN BARS DEPEND UPON THE POSITION THEY OCCUPY, FROM THE BOTTOM TO THE TOP.

7TH POSITION = 64.000.000 (3.200.000 × 20)
6TH POSITION = 3.200.000 (160.000 × 20)
5TH POSITION = 160.000 (8.000 × 20)
4TH POSITION = 8.000 (400 × 20)
3RD POSITION = 400 (1 × 20 × 20)
2ND POSITION = 20 (1 × 20)
1ST POSITION = 1 (UN.)

FOR INSTANCE.

2ND. POSITION
● ⇐ 1 × 20 = 20

● = 1 × 20 = 20 (SECOND POSITION)

●●●● = 4 × 20 = 80

⊞ ⇐ 1ST POSITION IS ZERO
20

5+5+5 = 15 (FIRST POSITION)
35

= 5
85

PRACTICE WITH THE PAGINATION OF THIS BOOK.

···
···· 6A

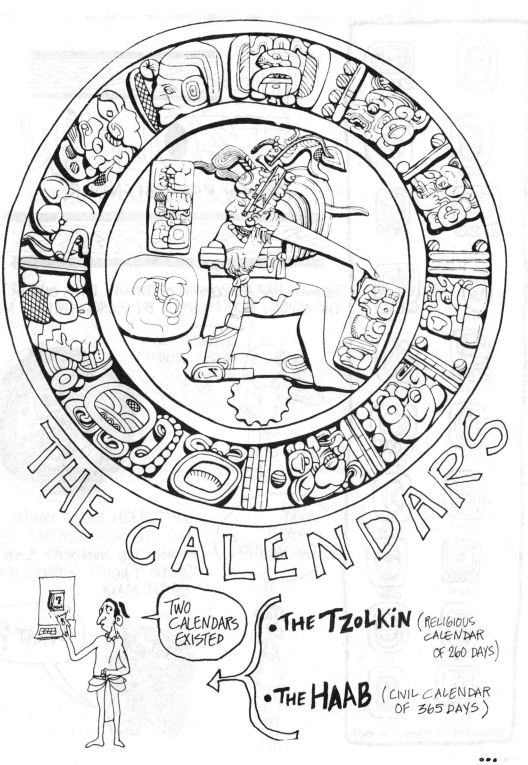

THE CALENDARS

TWO CALENDARS EXISTED

- THE **TZOLKIN** (RELIGIOUS CALENDAR OF 260 DAYS)

- THE **HAAB** (CIVIL CALENDAR OF 365 DAYS)

THE TZOLKIN
OR SACRED CALENDAR

THE MAYA HAD A SUCCESION OF TWENTY DAYS, ONE AFTER THE OTHER, REPRESENTED BY HIEROGLYPHICAL MEAN

WOULDN'T IT BE BETTER, MONDAY TUESDAY... ETC?

WHAT ABOUT THE MONTHS?

THE TZOLKIN, LACKED MONTHS. IT HAD 260 DAYS, FORMED BY ADDING THE NUMBERS 1 TO 13 TO THE TWENTY HIEROGLIPHS OF THE MAYA.

WHAT?

Ik
Eb
Akbal
Ben
Kan
Ix
Chicchan
Men
Cimi
Cib
Manik
Caban
Lamat
Eznab
Muluc
Cauac
Oc
Ahau
Chuen
Imix

HIEROGLYPS FOR THE 20 DAYS OF THE MONTH.

'EACH DAY POSSESED A NUMBER!

LIKE THIS:

1. IK
2. AKBAL
3. KAN
4. CHICCAN
5. CIMÍ
6. MANIK
7. LAMAT
8. MULUC
9. OC
10. CHUEN
11. EB
12. BEN
13. IX
14 ...

SINCE THEY HAD THIRTEEN NUMBERS ONLY, BUT TWENTY NAMES.

AT THIS MOMENT, THEY STARTED AGAIN WITH THE NUMBER ONE, AND A DIFFERENT NAME.

1. MEN
2. CIB AND ETCETERAS.

MULTIPLY TWENTY NAMES BY 13 NUMBERS AND YOU'LL HAVE 260 DAYS, THE TOTAL DAYS OF THE RELIGIOUS CALENDAR.

THEREFORE THE SAME COMBINATION NAME-NUMBER NEEDS 260 DAYS TO REPEAT ITSELF

✳ AS YOU CAN SEE BELOW.

TABLE OF THE COMPUTATION OF DAYS. RELIGIOUS CALENDAR.

IK	1	8	2	9	3	10	4	11	5	12	6	13	7
AKBAL	2	9	3	10	4	11	5	12	6	13	7	1	8
KAN	3	10	4	11	5	12	6	13	7	1	8	2	9
CHICCHAN	4	11	5	12	6	13	7	1	8	2	9	3	10
CIMI	5	12	6	13	7	1	8	2	9	3	10	4	11
MANIK	6	13	7	1	8	2	9	3	10	4	11	5	12
LAMAT	7	1	8	2	9	3	10	4	11	5	12	6	13
MOLUC	8	2	9	3	10	4	11	5	12	6	13	7	1
OC	9	3	10	4	11	5	12	6	13	7	1	8	2
CHUEN	10	4	11	5	12	6	13	7	1	8	2	9	3
EB	11	5	12	6	13	7	1	8	2	9	3	10	4
BEN	12	6	13	7	1	8	2	9	3	10	4	11	5
IX	13	7	1	8	2	9	3	10	4	11	5	12	6
MEN	1	8	2	9	3	10	4	11	5	12	6	13	7
CIB	2	9	3	10	4	11	5	12	6	13	7	1	8
CABAN	3	10	4	11	5	12	6	13	7	1	8	2	9
EZNAB	4	11	5	12	6	13	7	1	8	2	9	3	10
CAUAC	5	12	6	13	7	1	8	2	9	3	10	4	11
AHAU	6	13	7	1	8	2	9	3	10	4	11	5	12
IMIX	7	1	8	2	9	3	10	4	11	5	12	6	13

THE **TZOLKIN** WAS THE BETTER KNOW CALENDAR IN CENTRAL AMERICA. THE PEOPLE ALSO USED IT.

13 - MANIK
4 - MULUK
10 - CAUAC...
WHAT EVER THEIR NAMES ARE...

THE CARGO IS ALWAYS ON ME

DAYLY LIFE WAS GOVERNED BY THE **TZOLKIN**, ALSO KNOWN AS "COUNT OF DAYS"

BY MEANS OF THE TZOLKIN, THE TIME OF BURNING AND SOWING WAS SPECIFIED.

AND THE WARS!

FATE AND DESTINY OF THE MAYA INDIVIDUAL WAS DETERMINED AT THE MOMENT OF BIRTH, BY THE TZOLKING DAY HE WAS BORN.

THE CIVIL OR HAAB CALENDAR.

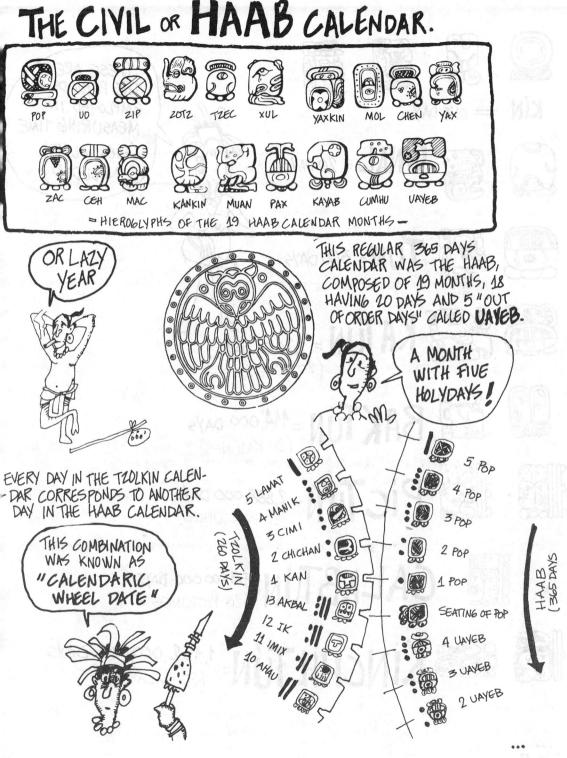

HIEROGLYPHS OF THE 19 HAAB CALENDAR MONTHS

POP · UO · ZIP · ZOTZ · TZEC · XUL · YAXKIN · MOL · CHEN · YAX

ZAC · CEH · MAC · KANKIN · MUAN · PAX · KAYAB · CUMHU · UAYEB

OR LAZY YEAR

THIS REGULAR 365 DAYS CALENDAR WAS THE HAAB, COMPOSED OF 19 MONTHS, 18 HAVING 20 DAYS AND 5 "OUT OF ORDER DAYS" CALLED **UAYEB**.

A MONTH WITH FIVE HOLYDAYS!

EVERY DAY IN THE TZOLKIN CALENDAR CORRESPONDS TO ANOTHER DAY IN THE HAAB CALENDAR.

THIS COMBINATION WAS KNOWN AS "CALENDARIC WHEEL DATE"

TZOLKIN (260 DAYS)

5 LAMAT
4 MANIK
3 CIMI
2 CHICHAN
1 KAN
13 AKBAL
12 IK
11 IMIX
10 AHAU

HAAB (365 DAYS)

5 POP
4 POP
3 POP
2 POP
1 POP
SEATING OF POP
4 UAYEB
3 UAYEB
2 UAYEB

KIN = ONE DAY

VINAL = 20 DAYS

TUN = 360 DAYS

KATÚN = 7,200 DAYS
(20 TUNES)

BAKTÚN = 114,000 DAYS
(20 KATUNES)

PICTÚN = 2,888,000 DAYS
(20 BAKTUNES)

CALABTÚN = 57 600 000 DAYS
(20 PICTUNES).

KINCHILTÚN = 1,152,000,000 DAYS
(20 CALABTUNES).

THESE ARE THE PERIODS EMPLOYED IN MEASURING TIME (HIEROGLYPH INCLUDED)

ARTS AND CRAFTS

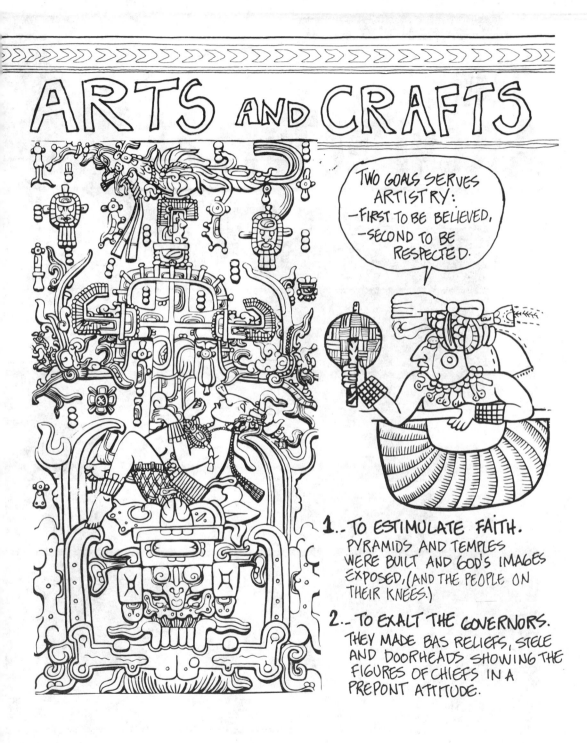

TWO GOALS SERVES ARTISTRY:
- FIRST TO BE BELIEVED,
- SECOND TO BE RESPECTED.

1.. TO ESTIMULATE FAITH. PYRAMIDS AND TEMPLES WERE BUILT AND GOD'S IMAGES EXPOSED, (AND THE PEOPLE ON THEIR KNEES.)

2.. TO EXALT THE GOVERNORS. THEY MADE BAS RELIEFS, STELE AND DOORHEADS SHOWING THE FIGURES OF CHIEFS IN A PREPONT ATTITUDE.

The Architecture

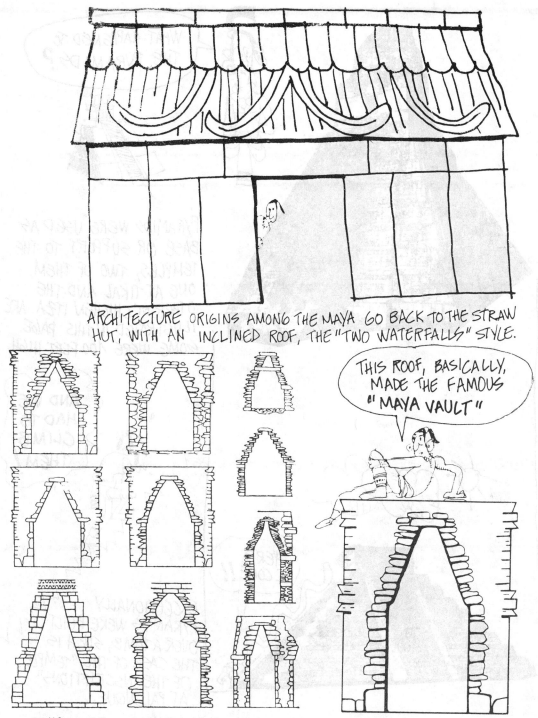

ARCHITECTURE ORIGINS AMONG THE MAYA GO BACK TO THE STRAW HUT, WITH AN INCLINED ROOF, THE "TWO WATERFALLS" STYLE.

THIS ROOF, BASICALLY, MADE THE FAMOUS "MAYA VAULT"

EXAMPLES OF "MAYA VAULT" OR FALSE ARCH.

WHAT HAPPENED TO THE PYRAMIDS?

PYRAMIDS WERE USED AS BASE OR SUPPORT TO THE TEMPLES, TWO OF THEM, ONE AT TIKAL AND THE OTHER AT CHICHEN ITZA ARE ILUSTRATED IN THIS PAGE. SOME WERE 100 FEET HIGH.

AND WE HAD TO CLIMB THEM!

HERE I COME!!

EXCEPTIONALLY PYRAMIDS WERE BUILT OVER A TOMB, SUCH IS THE CASE OF THE "TEMPLE OF THE INSCRIPTIONS" AT PALENQUE.

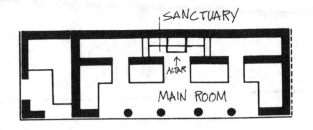

SANCTUARY

↑ ALTAR

MAIN ROOM

THIS WAS THE HOUSE OF A NOBLE MAN

AND ALSO RICH

STONE MADE, WITH A LEVELED ROOF BUILT WITH WOODEN BEAMS COVERED BY 12 INCHES OF MUD OR CLAY. WE STILL IGNORE THE HEIGHT OF THIS TYPE OF HOUSES

0 2 4 6 8
METROS

THE FACADE OF THESE BUILDINGS VARY ACCORDINGLY WITH THE MAYA REGIONS, ALLOWING TO RECOGNIZE THE DIFFERENT ARCHITECTURAL STYLES, WHICH ARE:

- • THE ANCIENT PETEN
- • THE PUUL
- • THE CHICHEN
- • THE CHENES
- • THE RIO BEC (BEC RIVER)

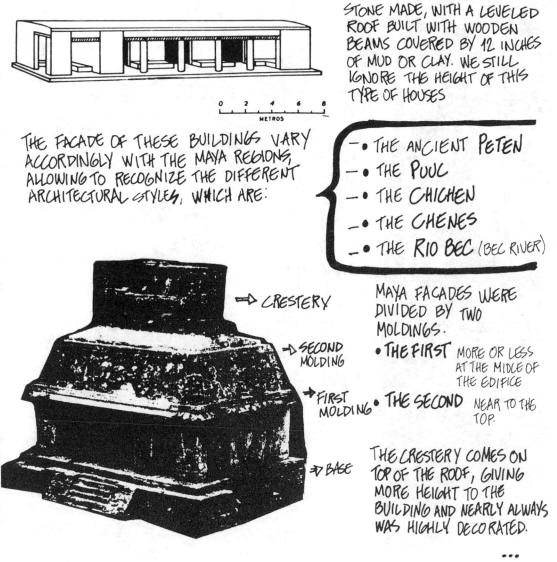

→ CRESTERY

→ SECOND MOLDING

→ FIRST MOLDING

→ BASE

MAYA FACADES WERE DIVIDED BY TWO MOLDINGS.
• THE FIRST MORE OR LESS AT THE MIDLE OF THE EDIFICE
• THE SECOND NEAR TO THE TOP.

THE CRESTERY COMES ON TOP OF THE ROOF, GIVING MORE HEIGHT TO THE BUILDING AND NEARLY ALWAYS WAS HIGHLY DECORATED.

•••

SCULPTURE

YOU JUST HAVE TO ANALIZE THE SCULPTURES TO KNOW WHO WERE THE MASTERS.

STUDYING THE MAYA SCULPTURE IT'S EASY TO CHECK THE RELIGIOUS AND CIVIL TRAITS OF THE RULING MINORITY.

FOUR WERE THE THEMES OF MAYA SCULPTURE:

ONE: REPRESENTATION OF GODS

TWO: OFFERINGS PRESENTATION

THREE: IMPORTANT PEOPLE ACTING AS MASTERS.

FOUR: ILL DEFINED SOCIAL CLASS PEOPLE ALWAYS APPEARING AS VICTIMS.

1 - STONE EXTRACTION

SCULPTURE WAS A JOB DONE WITH THESE MATERIALS:

- **LIMESTONE**
- **SANDSTONE**
- **ANDESITE** (VOLCANIC STONE USED ONLY AT **COPAN**)
- **WOOD** - USED IN ENGRAVED DOOR HEADS.
- **CLAY** - TO MODEL IDOLS IN THE FORM OF THURIBLES
- **STUCCO** - UTILIZED IN DECORATING BUILDINGS (BUILDING DECORATION).

2 - TRANSPORTING THE STONE

3 - LIFTING UP THE STONE

4 - ENGRAVING THE STONE

PAINTING

THE MAYA PAINTING WAS USED TO DECORATE WALLS, CERAMICS AND CODICES.

MOST DIFFICULT ARE THE ADORNMENTS THESE GUYS SPORT.

COLORS, OBTAINED FROM MINERALS AND VEGETA-
-BLES, WERE:

RED, TAKEN OUT FROM HEMALITES.

YELLOW, FROM A CLAY

BLACK, FROM COAL, AND.

BLUE, I DON'T KNOW.

THEY COMBINE EXQUISITELY THE DIFFERENTS SHADES OF THESE COLORS.

MAYA PAINTINGS WE KNOW ARE DATED FROM EARLY CLASSIC TO LATE POST-CLASSIC (V TO XV CENTURIES AD.) BONAMPAK EXHIBITS SOME OF THESE BEAUTIFUL PAINTINGS.

CERAMICS

DURING THE **PRE-CLASSIC** PERIOD CERAMIC DECORATION CONSISTED IN MAKING INCISIONS ON THE CLAY WITH ANY SHARP OBJECT.

WE ALSO USED OUR NAILS.

DURING THE **PROTOCLASSIC**, DECORATION COMBINING TWO COLORS USING SIMPLE GEOMETRICAL FORMS APPEARED. DURING THE **CLASSIC**, ALL THE COLORS ARE USED, DRAWING STYLIZED ANIMALS, HIEROGLYPHIC INSCRIPTIONS, RELIGIOUS SYMBOLS AND PERSONS.

DURING THE **POST CLASSIC** ORANGE CERAMICS APPEAR AND NEW FORMS: PLUMBED FINISH, CARVED OR STAMPED.

LA LAPIDARY

THE LAPIDARY ART OF THE MAYA MAY BE OBSERVED IN JADE CARVINGS DONE DURING THE **PRECLASSIC** PERIOD.

THE RENOWN **LEYDEN PLAQUE,** ONE OF THE FIRST OBJECTS CARVED, DATED 320 AD. IS A PIECE 9 INCHES LONG

MOST OF THESE OBJECTS WERE THE EXCLUSIVE USE OF RICH OR IMPORTANT PEOPLE WHO DEMANDED VERY MUCH EMBELLISHMENT, LIKE DIADEMS, CROWNS, ETC.

AND SEVERAL ETC.

OTHER ARTS MAYA DEVELOPED WERE.

- LITERATURE
- THEATER
- MOSAIC
- WEAVING.

MUSIC
(LA BAMBA!)

MAYA MUSIC IS
PENTAFONIC
(FIVE TONES) AS
USED BY MANY
ANCIENT CULTURES.

LUCY IN THE SKY
WITH DIAMONDS?
I DON'T BELIEVE
I CAN PLAY
IT!

THIS MUSIC IS MORE RYTHM THAN
HARMONY AND IS TIED TO SINGING
AND DANCING.

GLUC-GLUC-
GLUC-

THERE WERE MANY WIND INSTRUMENTS.

SPECIALLY FOR THE HEAT IN APRIL AND MAY.

THEY HAD LONG AND SLINE TRUMPETS.

THERE WERE ALSO SEA SHELLS THAT MADE A SHARP SOUND.

THEY HAD FLAUTS AND WHISTLES AND OTHER TYPE OF INSTRUMENTS THEY USED FRECUEN-TLY, LIKE COPPER JINGLES BONE OR SHELL SCRAPERS, AND THE TAMBOU-RINES MADE OF DRIED BUBBLE FRUITS OR COOKED CLAY.

LET THE RATTLE SING!

THEY HAD WIND AND PERCUSSION INSTRUMENTS.

ZACATLÁN

FOR THE TAM-TAM THEY HAD THE ZACATLAN

THE ZACATLAN WAS A SORT OF BIG DRUM (SOMETIMES IT WAS MORE THAN A YARD HIGH), MADE FROM A HOLLOW-TRUNK WITH ONE OPENING ONLY.

IT WAS GENERALLY MADE FROM THE TRUNK OF THE ZAPOTE TREE WITH TWO FLAPS ON THE TOP CUT IN AN "H" FORM. EACH FLAP HAD A DIFFERENT SOUND. IT'S EXCELLENT RESONANCE WAS HEARED MILES AWAY

FOR THE TUM-TUM THE TUNKUL

WE ALSO HAD THE "TURTLE SHELL". FOR MUSIC WE HIT IT WITH STICKS OR WITH THE DEERS HORN.

THE (GULP!) SACRIFICES

THE MAYA ALWAYS SACRIFICED PEOPLE, BUT THE THING REALLY GOT HOT WITH THE INFLUENCE OF THE MEXICAS THAT ARRIVED FROM TULA.

THE VICTIMS WERE ALMOST ALWAYS WAR PRISONERS AND SPECIALLY NOBLE ENEMIES.

THE SLAVES WERE SACRIFICED WHEN THEIR MASTERS DECIDED. THE CHILDREN WHEN THEY WERE DONATED BY THEIR PARENTS OR WHEN THEY WERE SOLD BY KIDNAPPERS (THEIR JOB WAS TO SEARCH FOR VICTIMS) AND THERE WAS ALSO THE VOLUNTARY VICTIM. HIS PURPOSE WAS TO PERPETUATHE HIS MEMORY... (WHAT A WAY).

THE DIVING STYLE WAS FRECUENTLY USED. THE METHOD CONSISTED IN THROWING THE VICTIMS TO THE SACRED "CENOTE" (WATER HOLE AT CHICHEN ITZA).

WE SEND THEM TO **CHAAC** AND IN REPLY HE WATERED THE FIELDS.

PEOPLE WERE THROWN IN THE "CENOTE" TO CALM THE ANGER OF SOME GOD AND TO UNDERSTAND HIS WILL TROUGH THE TESTIMONY OF A SURVIVER

(THEY NEVER RECALLED A TESTIMONY)

....

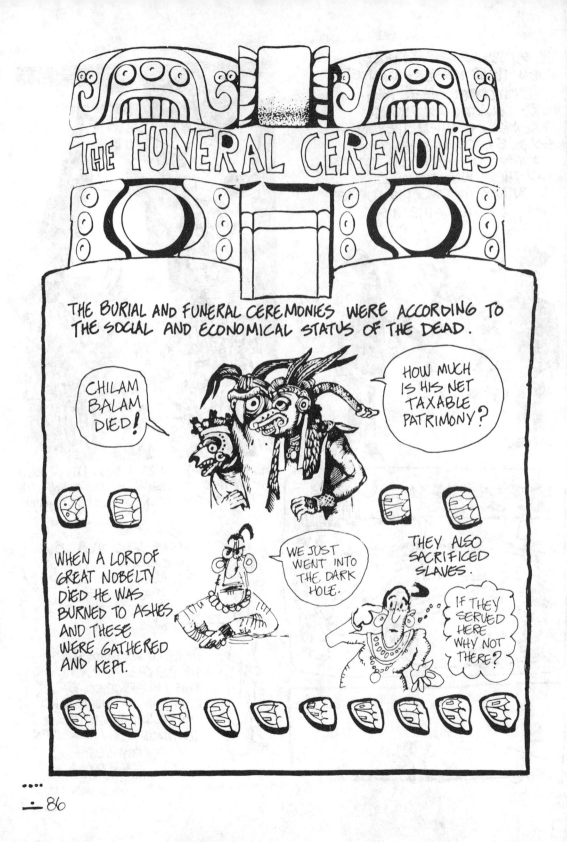

WELL, WELL... THERE GOES ANOTHER TOURIST.

WHEN A **MAYA** DIED THEY PREPARED HIM FOR BURIAL PUTTING A PASTE OF GRATED CORN IN HIS MOUTH (KEYEN) SO HE WOULDN'T DIE OF HUNGER DURING HIS VOYAGE.

FOR THE COMMON PEOPLE CORN, FOR US JADE COINS.

THE POPULACE WAS BURIED UNDER THE FLOOR OR IN THE BACKYARD OF THE HOUSE. (AFTERWARD THEY ABANDONED THE HOUSE).

SO MUCH NOISE AND AT THE END THEY ALL CROSS THE SAME ROAD.

THE AGRICULTURE

TO CULTIVATE CORN WAS FOR THE MAYA A SORT OF RELIGIOUS ACTIVITY.

EVERYTHING DEPENDED ON THIS OLD GUY.

THE CULTIVATING METHOD WAS PRIMITIVE: SINCE THEY DIDN'T HAVE MEANS TO PRACTICE THE ARTIFICIAL IRRIGATION, THE HARVEST DEPENDED ENTIRELY IN THE RAIN (ON MR. CHAAC, TO BE PRECISE).

THE OPERATION BEGAN WITH THE **FELLING** OF TREES.

TIMBER!!

...WHICH WAS DONE IN WINTER FROM DECEMBER TO FEBRUARY.

TAKE IT EASY WITH THE ECOLOGY MISTER.

THE FLAMES!

THE LAST DAYS OF MARCH OR THE FIRST OF APRIL, WHEN EVERY-THING WAS DRY, THEY BURNED THE FIELDS.

WHEN THE RAINS BROKE DOWN AT THE END OF MAY OR THE BEGINNING OF JUNE THEY PLANTED THE SEEDS.

THIS IS THE REAL WAY TO GET A WONDERFULL TAN.

WE USED THIS STICK, IT'S SHARP POINT WAS CALLED **XUL**

WITH THE FAMOUS **XUL** THEY MADE SMALL HOLES IN THE SOIL AND PLANTED THERE CORN GRAINS MIXED WITH PUMPKIN AND BEAN SEEDS.

THEY LOOKED FOR ANOTHER PRETTY PLOT OF LAND AND REPEATED THE OPERATION.

WHO CARES, WE HAVE MORE THAN ENOUGH LAND.

THE PLOT OF LAND HAD TO BE CHANGED OR THE CROP DIMINISHED.

AND THEN THERE WOULD BE NO "TORTILLAS" TO TRICK THE BELLY

GRAUNCH

NOT ONLY OF CORN LIVED THE MAYA.

THEY ALSO CULTIVATED:
- BLACK BEANS (XOCOL, TZAMÁ)
- CHILE (IX)
- CHAYA (CHAY)
- TOMATO (P'AC)
- SWEET POTATO (IZ)
- JICAMA (CHICAM)
- PUMPKIN (KUN XCA')
- YUCCA (TZIN)

AND FRUIT TREES?
- AVOCADO (ON)
- ANNONA (OP)
- PLUM TREE (AVAL)
- PAPAYA (PUT)
- NANCE (CHI')
- SAPOTE (YA)
- LONGAN (UAYUM)
- CHERIMOYA (DZALMUY)

FEEDING AND NUTRITION

DO YOU HAVE ANY DOUBT?

THE BASIC FOOD AMONG THE MAYA WAS THE **CORN!!**

COMPLEMENTED WITH SOME ANIMALS MEAT.

LET'S SEE:
- NATIVE TURKEY (TZO')
- THE TURTLEDOVE (MUCUY)
- THE DOVE (TZU TZU)
- SEVERAL TYPES OF DUCKS (CUTZHA')
AND A SORT OF UNHAIRED LITTLE DOG

THE MAYA ALSO HUNTED.

- THE DEER AND THE PHEASANT
- THE PIG (KITAM)
- THE RABBIT (THUL)
- THE ARMADILLO (UECH)
- THE QUAIL (BEECH)
- THE COX,
AND ANY OTHER ANIMAL THAT STEPED IN FRONT OF HIM, LIKE IGUANAS OR SNAKES.

HUNTING WAS NOT JUST "FUN AND GAMES"
THE MAYA ORGANIZED IT COMMUNALY.

THE BIRD IS FOR HE WHO WORKS FOR IT!

NOT EXACTLY! THE CAPTURE WAS DIVIDED AMONG ALL THE HUNTERS AND A PART WAS LEFT FOR THE BATAB.

GOOD GRIEF!

YOU HAD TO PAY BIRD-TAX!
(WOULD YOU BELIEVE IT?)

I LIKE T-BONE!

WHEN PRAY WAS SUFFI--CIENT THEY STAINED BLOOD ON TH FACE OF THEIR IDOLS. IF NOT, THE MAYA WHIPED THE HELL OUT OF THEIR IDOLS.

NOT EVEN A LITTLE DEER, YOU BASTARD!

HE WHO CAPTURED A DEER OR A PIG, DEMANDED WHAT HE LIKED MOST. THE REST WAS FOR THE OTHER HUNTERS.

THEY LIKED VERY MUCH, AND CONSUME WHEN POSSIBLE, FISH MEET. THE PUMPKIN WAS BOTH APPRECIATED AND RELEVANT TO THE MAYA DIET.

PUMPKIN IS PURE COLESTEROL!

HONEY WAS OVERUSED, PARTICULAR IN PREPARING A FUNNY LITTLE LIQUOR, DRANK IN ALL RITUAL AND CEREMONIES CALLED

BALCHÉ!

BALCHÉ

THE SAUCE, IS FOR YOU PLEASE

IN BANQUETS, THE MAYA ATE AND DRANK WITHOUT PITY. BUT IN DAYLY LIFE THEY WERE SOBER AND WELL GOVERNED.

CORN AGAIN?

CORN PREPARED IN THESE WAYS:
- TORTILLAS (UAH)
- ATOLE (ZA')
- POZOLE (KEYEM)
- TAMALES (MUXUBAAK)

AT DOWN, THE MAYA TOOK CORN DISSOLVED IN HOT WATER

WITH SALT AND CHILI!

SOMETIMES THEY DRANK TOASTED CORN, GRINDED AND DISSOLVED IN WATER.

TORTILLAS? THAT'S FOR THE RABBLE.

WE BREAKFEAST WITH CACAO!

WHILE WORKING UNDER 90 OR MORE DEGREES, THEY DRANK "POZOLE" A COMBINATION OF WATER AND CORN.

BACK HOME THE MAYA ATE THEIR ONLY REAL MEAL OF THE DAY (BREAKFAST, SUPPER, ALL IN ONE), COMPOSED OF TORTILLAS WITH SALT AND CHILI, A SPECIAL KIND OF BOILED BEANS AND A PUREE OR THICK SOUP MADE OF PUMPKIN.

PRODUCTION

PUT YOUR MONEY WERE YOUR MOUTH IS!

FOR THE MAYA, THE MAIN SOURCE OF REVENUES WAS THE **SALT**, USED AS MUCH FOR LOCAL CONSUMPTION AS FOR EXPORTATION.

SALT PAYS TRIBUTES AND TAXES, AND PRESERVES THE MEAT.

THE SALINES WERE COMMON PROPERTY.

WHO SAID "COMMON"? A PART WAS GIVEN TO THE MASTERS!

FOR CLOTH, THEY USED SEVERAL PLANTS AND TREES
- COTTON (TAMAM)
- POCHOTE (CHO, PIN)
- HENEQUEN (KI)
- SILKCOTTON TREE (YAX CHE)

PAPER WAS MADE OF THE COPO BARK

FROM THE **ZAPOTE** CAME THE **CHICLETS**, AND FOR THE **POOM** PERFUMED RESINS

ANOTHER IMPORTANT PRODUCE OF YUCATAN WAS THE **HONEY** THE ONE ELABORATED BY THE BEES. I MEAN.

BO. BEE.

THE COMMERCE

FOR THE MAYAS (AS FOR THE REST OF THE WORLD) TRADE WAS OF THE OUTMOST IMPORTANCE. TRANSPORTATION OF GOODS WERE CARRIED OUT BY PORTERS.

IT IS ALSO BELIEVED THAT A SORT OF MARITIME TRADE EXISTED AT THE END OF POST-CLASSIC PERIOD.

FOR BUSSINESS AND TRANSACTIONS THE LAW WAS THE **EXCHANGE.** THEY ALSO USED AS CURRENCY CACAO GRAINS, ALONG WITH JADE MARBLES, AND VERY RARE SEA SHELLS. **THE MONEY MAN!**

NO INFLATED GRAINS, NOR DEVALUATED SHELLS TO ME FOOLS! I WANT DOLLARS!

MAIN IMPORTS WERE: JADE, PRECIOUS FEATHERS, GOLD, SOME SHELLS AND CERAMIC AND POTTERY.

WITH GUATEMALA THEY EXCHANGED CACAO FOR MAYA SALT, HONEY, FABRICS AND SLAVES

AFFIRMATIVE SPECULATION - AT A GLOBAL LEVEL - MARKS THE INDEXATION PROCESS HELPED BY HIPERVALORATION OF INTERCONNECTED ARANCELS, ADDED TO THE INTRINGULIS, THE CONSUBSTANTIAL ONE, IS KEEPING INFLATION SO HIGH IT DOESN'T LET US GROW

WHO KNOWS. THE FACT IS I'M SITTING IN A PYLE OF SHIT!

MERCHANTS OF ALL KIND ABOUND. THE RICH, ARISTOCRATIC ONES ; THE WORRIED ONES (PLENY OF STRESS), THE BARELY SURVIVING ONES (PLENY OF DEBTS) AND THE BANKRUPT ONES (PLENY OF SHIT).

THE LAW

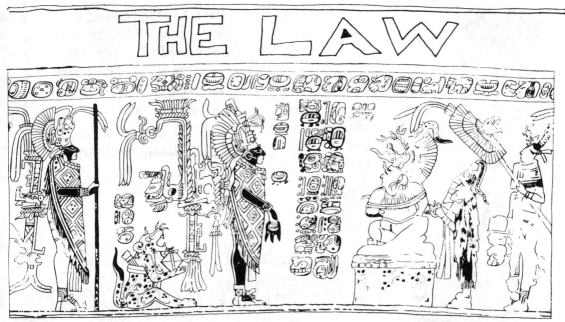

AMONG THE MAYA EXISTED THE COMMON LAW OR **CUSTOMAR** LAW, INGRAINED IN USES AND SOCIAL HABITS.

THE MATTER WAS A LITTLE BIT RIGID: SOME OFFENSES COST THE LIFE.

LITIGATIONS, LAWSUITS, CONTRACTS AND SEVERAL ETCETERAS WERE HELD **ORALLY**, PARTICIPATING JUDGES ATTORNEYS, LITIGANTS AND WITNESSES.

JUDGES RECEIVED PRESENTS DURING THE TRIAL.

IN SPITE OF THAT THEY CALLED THEMSELVES "IMPARTIALS"

ABOUT SEVENTEEN STABS, BUT UNINTENTIONAL.

THEY DISTINGUISHED BETWEEN DELICTS AND DEMEANORS, THE FIRST ONES BEING AGGRAVATED OFFENSES. THEY HAD NO PRISONS. DEATH OR FORCED LABOR WERE THE PUNISHMENT FOR THOSE PROVED GUILTY.

SLAVERY WAS A LEGAL SANCTION, AS MUCH AS TO SET THE GUILTY ONE TO THE OFFENDED HANDS, EVEN IN HOMICIDAL CASES. IT WAS SOCIAL VENGEANCE, NOT SOCIAL PROTECTION.

EYE BY EYE TOOTH BY TOOTH!

NOBODY WAS PUNISHED BECAUSE OF HIS DEBTS.

RELATIVES OF THE DEBTOR HAD TO PAY FOR HIM. BURGLARS WERE CONDEMNED TO GIVE BACK THE STOLEN THINGS OR SOMETHING OF THE SAME VALUE. IMPOSIBILITATED TO DO IT THEY PAYED WITH A TIME IN SALVERY.

ADULTERY, TREASON, ARSON, VIOLATION AND HOMICIDE RECEIVED THE DEATH PENALTY.

PRISONERS HAD THEIR ARMS TIED TO THE BACK AND A NECKLACE. AN EXTREME VILIFYING PUNISHMENT WAS TO CROP THE HAIR.

SOCIAL HABITS

♪♪ ROCK-A-BYE BABY ON THE TREE-TOP

THE MAYA CONSIDERED A BEAUTY TO HAVE THE HEAD DEFORMED AS IN THE PICTURE.

THIS CRANEAL DEFORMATION BEGAN THE FOURTH DAY AFTER BIRTH.

I WONDER WHY THEY CALL ME "WATER MELON HEAD"

THEY WERE ALSO DELIGHTED BY HAVING THEIR EYES SQUINT OR CROSSED.

¡AGU!

THE CHILD WAS SUSPENDED FROM THE HAIR AND ON THE FOREHEAD THEY PUT SEVERAL RUBBER-MARBLES THAT FORCED THE CHILD TO TWIST THE EYES.

DRESSING

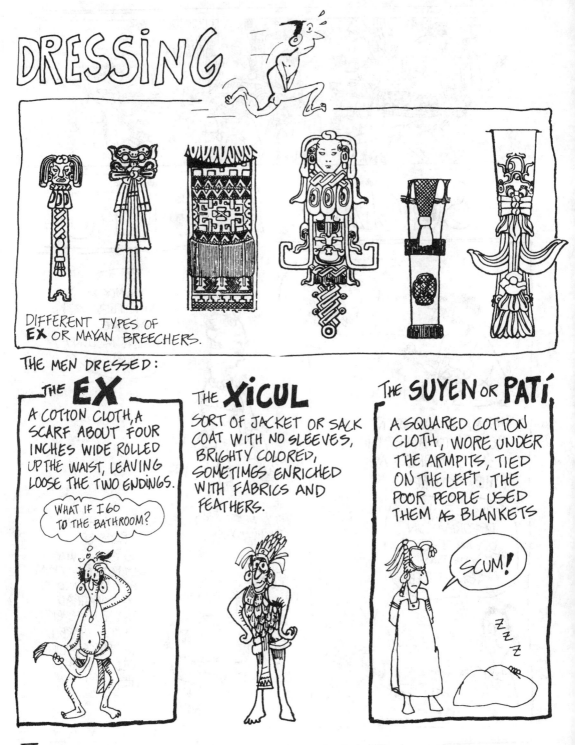

DIFFERENT TYPES OF **EX** OR MAYAN BREECHERS.

THE MEN DRESSED:

THE **EX**

A COTTON CLOTH, A SCARF ABOUT FOUR INCHES WIDE ROLLED UP THE WAIST, LEAVING LOOSE THE TWO ENDINGS.

WHAT IF I GO TO THE BATHROOM?

THE **XICUL**

SORT OF JACKET OR SACK COAT WITH NO SLEEVES, BRIGHTY COLORED, SOMETIMES ENRICHED WITH FABRICS AND FEATHERS.

THE **SUYEN** OR **PATÍ**

A SQUARED COTTON CLOTH, WORE UNDER THE ARMPITS, TIED ON THE LEFT. THE POOR PEOPLE USED THEM AS BLANKETS

SCUM!

ZZZ

I'D GIVE MY SOUL FOR A TANGA

→ HUIPIL

→ PIC

WOMEN WORE THE **HUIPIL**, A LOOSE GARMENT, LARGE AND WIDE, OPENED IN BOTH SIDES.

THE **PIC**, AN UNDERSKIRT WORE UNDER THE HUIPIL.

THEY ALSO WORE A SORT OF BRA, A PIECE OF COARSE COTTON CLOTH TIED UNDER THE ARMPIT.

MEN AND WOMEN WORE THE **XANAB** OR DEER SKIN SANDAL, OF DIFFERENT FORMS AN SIZES (ACCORDING TO YOUR BUDGET, OF COURSE).

NO PROBLEM WITH OUR HAIRDRESSERS, MAN!

THE COIFFURE WAS AN ORNAMENT DENOTING LINEAGE. IT HAD AN OSIER FRAME COVERED BY FEATHERS.

WHAT ABOUT THE NAMES?

GIVING A NAME TO A MAYA WAS A FOUR STEP PROCESS.

1. PAAL KABÁ.

YOUR NAME IS JOE AND THAT'S IT.

IT WAS EQUIVALENT TO OUR CHRISTIAN NAME. THESE WERE TAKEN MOSTLY FROM THOSE OF ANIMALS OR PLANTS.

-DONKEY JONES- FOR EXAMPLE

THIS CHRISTIAN NAME, LET'S SAY CHUY (HAWK) OR KEH (DEER), HAD A PREFIX:

AH WHEN THE NAMED WAS MAS-CULINE.

IX OR **X** WHEN FEMENINE. AFTER THE PAAL KABA THE FATHER'S NAME CAME.

NAMES LIKE THIS RESULTED:

AH CHUY MAY
(MALE) (HAWK)

IX KEH HUCHIM
(FEMALE) (DEER)

2. NAAL KABA'

AFTER MARRIAGE, THE **PAAL-KABA** WAS SUBSTITUED BY THE **NAAL-KABA**, IN WHICH THE FIRST WORD (THE PREFIX) **NA**—MEANING MOTHER— PRECEDES THE COMMON NAME, AFTER WHICH THE PATERNAL SURNAME COMES.

MY NAME? SINGLE OR MARRIED?

- NACHI COCOM
- NA POOT XIU
- NA CHAN CHEL

(PREFIX) (COMMON NAME) (PATERNAL SURNAME)

3. COCO KABA'

NOTHING LESS THAN THE NICKNAME. EVERY MAYA WAS GIVEN ONE

BLACK FOOT!

FOR INSTANCE:
- AH XOCHIL ICH
(OWL'S FACE)

4. PROFESIONAL NAME.

THE NAME OF THE GUY'S OCUPATION.

FOR INSTANCE:

- **CHILAM BALAM**
(THE SEER BALAM)

- **AH KIN CHI**
(CHI, THE PRIEST)

AND WITH THIS,
WE PITCH THE LAST
STONE OF THESE
"MAYA ON THE ROCKS"
UPON WHICH THE
AUTHOR WALKED
— BAREFOOT UNDER
THE BURNNING
SUN— TO BRING
TO YOU, DEAR
READER, A SHALLOW
VISION OF THESE
PEOPLE, THE DEER
AND THE PHEASANT
PEOPLE, (ALTHOUGHT
DEER THERE ARE NO MORE,
AND PHESEANTS NEITHER).
AS A LAST WORD
LET US REPEAT WHAT
THE SLAVE AH TZAB
KUMUN TOLD TO HIS
MASTER HAVING HIS
TONGUE OFF:

"U XUL IN T'AN LA'
(THIS IS MY LAST WORD)

AND MINE TOO!

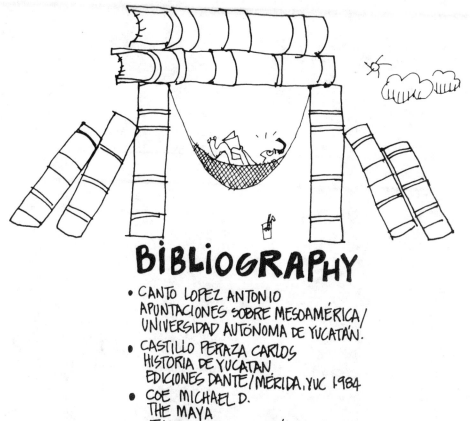

BIBLIOGRAPHY

- CANTO LOPEZ ANTONIO
  APUNTACIONES SOBRE MESOAMÉRICA/
  UNIVERSIDAD AUTÓNOMA DE YUCATÁN.
- CASTILLO PERAZA CARLOS
  HISTORIA DE YUCATAN
  EDICIONES DANTE/MÉRIDA. YUC 1.984
- COE MICHAEL D.
  THE MAYA
  THAMES AND HUDSON/LONDON 1.984
- GALLENKAMP CHARLES
  LOS MAYAS
  EDITORIAL DIANA/MÉXICO 1.976
- MORLEY SYLVANUS
  LA CIVILZACIÓN MAYA.
  FONDO DE CULTURA ECONÓMICA/MEX 1985
- SODI DEMETRIO
  LOS MAYAS
  PANORAMA /MEXICO/1982
- THOMPSON J. ERIC
  GRANDEZA Y DECADENCIA DE LOS MAYAS
  FONDO DE CULTURA ECONÓMICA/MEX 1985
- THOMPSON J. ERIC
  HISTORIA Y RELIGIÓN DE LOS MAYAS
  SIGLO XXI /MÉXICO 1.985
- TURNER WILSON
  MAYA DESIGN
  USA /1.980.

La edición consta de 2,000 ejemplares.
Impreso en mayo de 1997 en **Litoarte, S.A. de C.V.**,
San Andrés Atoto No. 21-A, Col. Ind. Atoto,
Naucalpan, 53519, encuadernado en
Sevilla Editores, S.A. de C.V.
Vicente Guerrero No. 38,
San Antonio Zomeyucan,
Naucalpan, 53750,
Edo. de México.